Wheat and Weeds and the Wolf of Gubbio

Stories and Prayers for People who Pray and for People who Don't

Graziano Marcheschi

*Illustrations by
Stephen Titra*

Sheed & Ward

Copyright© 1994 by Graziano Marcheschi

Sheed & Ward™ is a service of The National Catholic Reporter Publishing Company.

Library of Congress Cataloguing-in-Publication Data in Process
Marcheschi, Graziano
ISBN: 1-55612-661-1

Published by: Sheed & Ward
115 E. Armour Blvd.
P.O. Box 419492
Kansas City, MO 64141

To order, call: (800) 333-7373

Cover and illustrations by Stephen Titra ©1994

*C*ontents

Sparks

Dreams of the Kingdom

DEDICATION

For Nancy. I've waited a long time to give this book to you as a feeble thanks for all you are. I've found a creed I want to learn to live, but you in many ways have already shown me how:

> I would be true, for there are those who trust me;
> I would be pure, for there are those who care;
> I would be strong, for there is much to suffer;
> I would be brave, for there is much to dare.[1]

For the trust and care you've given me, for strength in my suffering and courage to brave the things I feared . . . *grazie, Anzia bella.* I saved my best for you.

---

1. Howard Arnold Walter (1883-1918) *My Creed.*

INTRODUCTION

FIVE WISHES

1. Playing Host

You hear an old song and the face of a lost loved one suddenly appears, and in the space of the song the loved one grabs your loneliness by the collar and sends it out the door.

You stand before a painting and the peaceful landscape calls you in—or a scene of violent pain holds you in thrall—and for a minute that's longer than eternity you enter the serenity, or you rage and grieve along with the picture's tortured souls.

You read a piece of poetry and for the span of a minute—or an hour—you find a space to sit and listen to the sound of naked joy, or to stare into the face of unfathomable grief.

More than anything else, that's what good art does: not answer questions or set agendas, but create space—space to laugh, to mourn, and to wonder who and how and why we are.

In my writing I have made many mistakes. Perhaps the greatest was thinking that I had to provide answers—pat ones if possible. Often I would start a piece that would cruise along quite well, but just about the time when I would think it should be moving toward an ending, I'd get stuck. "What is this poem saying," I would ask myself. And when I couldn't answer, I would panic. I'd try to hatch an insight, a lesson, that would give the piece some meaning and some purpose. Sometimes it worked, but more often I'd find myself sitting on cracked and empty shells.

When I read other people's poetry I saw that usually it didn't offer answers or clever insights either. And though I couldn't say just what it did, I knew it did more than offer nice rhythms and pretty images.

I began realizing how often I went back to familiar poetry the way I might go back to a favorite park bench—just to have a place to sit and be, and feel a certain way. These favorite poems gave me a place to be human. They provided space to laugh. Space to mourn. Space to be angry, to surrender, to hope. Songs, I realized, also did that for me. They gave me a place to live— for a time. I didn't expect to find "answers" there; I was just glad for the space. And in those spaces poetry and music made for me I often found a table set with rich, nourishing food. No one had

to tell me to sit and dine. It was obvious. That's what I was
there to do. And so I feasted.

That kind of experience, I realized, was routine in my life. Probably it happens regularly in your life, too. Artists are the people
responsible for that. They are hosts who create "a habitable world
in which all of us can live."[1] When we watch a fine film or listen
to a profound piece of music we find ourselves entering a "human
space" where we can engage powerful emotions. And somehow
in that space we find ourselves nourished. The hope, the joy, the
vision of a renewed and better world embodied in and expressed
by the work of art become the food on which we feast. Not
simple, pat answers. Not lectures and lessons. But a place where
emotions can be engaged, where visions can be seen, where hopes
can be expressed, strength found, and human beings can live. A
world where God's love can make "all things new," where healing
and wholeness are the norm, becomes a possibility. Even when
the artist does not, cannot, believe that such a world is possible in
this life, good art points with hope to that possibility.

That's the artist's gift. And the first of my five wishes is that
these pieces might do the same. So a suggestion: read slowly.
Sit inside each piece and take the space it offers.

2. Saints and Poets, Maybe

In Thornton Wilder's *Our Town* young Emily Webb is granted a
single day on which to return to earth after her death. She
chooses her twelfth birthday. As her family members buzz around
her in busy preparations for her birthday celebration, Emily
notices all the little things which, in life, had blurred right past
her. "It goes so fast," she says. "We don't have time to look at
one another. I didn't realize. So all that was going on and we
never noticed."

At one point, when Emily can't find her hair ribbon, her mother's
advice announces the play's theme: "Just keep your eyes open
dear, that's all." But, by play's end, Emily's wide-open eyes con-
vince her that human beings are "just blind people." Finally, a

---

1. I am indebted to Nathan Mitchell, OSB, for some of these insights regarding
the artist as host, and for the language which names my experience and brings to
conscious expression what I had "known" only on an intuitive level. His powerful
and poetic articulation of the notion of art creating space is found in "The
Musician as Minister," first published in *Pastoral Music,* Vol. 4, No. 6,
August-September 1980, pp. 27-31, 39-41.

tearful Emily asks, "Do any human beings ever realize life while they live it?—every, every minute?" The Stage Manager who narrates the play answers "No." But after a pause he adds, "the saints and poets, maybe—they do some."

That's another wish for what this book might do: call forth the saint and poet in each of us. Or, to put it more prosaically, and echo Mrs. Webb's advice, to remind us just to keep our eyes open.

Father John Shea offers the same advice when he talks about theological reflection:

> It is harder to learn from life than you think. Life is a series of fragmented activities. We need to pay attention in order to learn from life. There is more going on than you know. Divine reality has been active in you. Being faithful is learning to respond to what is given—the gift of life—*while it is being given.*[2]

Perhaps reading a book like this can help slow things down a little—at least enough to enable us to realize a bit more of life *as it happens.*

3. Can We Pray?

In his powerful (yet too little known) book, *The Mass in Time of Doubt*, Ralph Keifer claims that "authentic prayer is scarcely possible today unless it is tempered by serious doubt."[3] It is not difficult to agree with him. Look around, and it is easy to see that many Christians have more questions than answers, more doubt than certainty. God appears silent on so many fronts that one might well conclude that God is either powerless or uncaring regarding human struggle and pain. So a question arises: Can people of doubt who protest the silence of God also be people of prayer? Some might offer a quick "No," (after all, prayer demands trust and solid faith!), but honest people must concede that dissent and disillusionment are not infrequent companions even of people who pray. Karl Rahner lends a perspective that is helpful here. As quoted by Keifer, Rahner suggests where we might find the author of all prayer, the Holy Spirit, at work in human lives:

2. From a lecture presented to the Lay Ministry Formation Program, Archdiocese of Chicago, Sept. 27, 1986.

3. Ralph Keifer, *The Mass in Time of Doubt* (Washington, DC: National Association of Pastoral Musicians, 1983), p. vi.

When a single sustaining hope enables us to face coura-
geously both the enthusiastic highs and the depressing lows
of earthy existence; when a responsibility freely accepted
continues to be carried out, though it no longer bears any
visible promise of success or usefulness; when a human
being not only experiences but willingly accepts the last free
choice of his death; when the moment of death is recognized
as a fulfillment of the promise of life; when we no longer
have any proof of the total value of our life's actions, and
yet have the strength to view them as positive in God's
eyes; when the fragmentary experience of love, beauty and
joy can quite simply be experienced as a continued promise
of love, beauty and joy; when the bitter and disappointing
and trying events of every day are endured serenely and
patiently even to the last day, sustained by a strength whose
source is forever elusive; when one dares to pray in silence
and darkness and knows that he is heard, without thereafter
being able to discuss or dispute his answer; when one delib-
erately embarks upon total retreat and can experience this as
true victory; when falling can truly be called standing; when
lack of hope can be seen as a mysterious kind of consolation
(without indulgence in cheap comfort); when one has
reached the point of trusting all his certainty and all his
doubts to the silent and encompassing mystery that he now
loves above his personal achievements . . . This is where we
truly find God and his liberating grace, where we experience
what we Christians call the Holy Spirit, where the difficult
but unavoidable experiences of life are welcomed with joy
as challenges to our freedom and not as fearful specters
against which we try to barricade ourselves in a hell of false
freedom to which we are then damned.[4]

These experiences of ambiguity and confusion, these paradoxical
life moments that may seem to stretch and even snap our faith,
can be, in fact, our times of deepest prayer. We don't pray
despite our confusion and doubt, we pray and in and through—and
because—of them.

Wish number three, then, is that the stories in this book truthfully
name some of those moments of confusing grace and even lead to
cherishing them as moments of divine encounter.

---

4. *Ibid.* p. 21-22.

4. Burning Hearts

My mother warned me when I was young, "Keep the company of fools, and you'll soon become one." I did both. You see, two of the best companions I've ever encountered on my journey were the disciples on the road to Emmaus. What fools *they* were. They couldn't even recognize the Lord when he stared them in the face. And like the Emmaus disciples, I too have failed to recognize the Lord (he wears such great disguises!) in most of the thousands of encounters of my life.

But one dramatic moment turned the disciples' foolishness into Godly wisdom. At dinner, over broken bread, they remembered the heart that had been burning within them, and realized who had set it afire.

This story of the disciples' walk to Emmaus is, I believe, the foundation of all story theology. Story theology does nothing more than help us *remember* and make us *suspicious*: it helps us remember the burning heart moments of our lives so that we realize that never on our journey did we walk alone; and it makes us suspicious that the one who had and still accompanies us on the road is the very Lord we seek.

The disciples' eyes were opened when they broke bread with Jesus. Suddenly they remembered the road—and the fire in their hearts. And just as suddenly they realized that their encounter with the Holy had begun not when they sat at the table, but as they walked the road. In fact, they were so overwhelmed by the realization that the *whole day* had been an experience of the Holy, that they didn't even seem to notice Jesus' sudden disappearance from the table.

Like the Emmaus disciples we, too, daily, walk with strangers we fail to recognize. But later, sometimes much later, we look back and become suspicious.

Number four wish: that these stories will awaken memories of the holy, burning hearts moments of life; that it might spark an awareness of the many and convincing disguises God takes on; and that it make you suspicious of the true identity of those well-disguised strangers who have walked through your life or stood at your side.

5. The Rhythm that Makes Life Human

We live. Things happen to us. Then, if we're lucky, we stop to think about them. Tad Guzie says that's the first step in a cycle that's necessary for life to be truly human. The things that happen are raw life experience. But raw experience is not the same as *lived* experience. Only we can turn raw experience into lived experience, and to do that we must reflect on our experiences and find their significance for our lives.[5]

Then we tell a story. "When an experience comes to have significance related to our lives," says Guzie, "we put it into story form. Storytelling is our most spontaneous and basic way of naming an experience."[6] But the process of telling our own story always goes on in front of a backdrop of some larger cultural story or "myth." There are many we could use for this purpose, but we choose one story because we find that it, more than the others, helps us make meaning in our lives.

For Christians, that myth is the story of God's love as embodied in the history of the Jewish people and in the life, death and resurrection of Jesus. It is that story that gives meaning to the otherwise random events of our lives; that story alone that can help us give a cohesive shape to our otherwise raw experience.

That, of course, is not a put-down of other people's stories or myths. Rather, it is a confessional statement. As Christians we must be people of memory. Stanley Hauerwas points out that we are a "story-formed" community; we know who we are because of the story we cherish and tell. We value that story not because it tells us what to do, but because it reminds us who we are to *be*.[7] However, we can be shaped by our story only if we know it, and we will know it only if we *love* it. And unless we love our story, passionately—so passionately that it begins to evoke dreams of what might be—we will not be people who are faithful to the Judeo-Christian tradition from which we spring.

My fifth wish: that these stories be bridges—that they connect you with *the* story by helping you see that every page of the Jesus story tells the story of your life, and that every day of your life retells the Jesus story in new and compelling images.

---

5. Tad Guzie, *The Book of Sacramental Basics* (New York: Paulist Press, 1981), p. 9-12.

6. Ibid, p. 12.

7. Stanley Hauerwas, *The Peaceable Kingdom* (Notre Dame: University of Notre Dame Press, 1983), pp. 17-34.

ABOUT THE BOOK

These Stories are True

I would like to offer no explanation (the "Did it really happen" kind) regarding the truth of these stories, except to say that some happened to me, some to people I know, and a few to no one in particular. Sometimes the writing occurred in close proximity with the actual events, and sometimes years later. Occasionally the muse dictated the words faster than I could write them, but other times I cast a bucket into a near-dry well and pulled them up one-at-a-time. Sometimes I knew how the story ended before I started writing, but many times only after I'd finished.

Which stories are "historically" true and which are "made up" seems insignificant since, if the stories work, they all achieve a level of truthfulness. Every writer's vocation is to tell the truth, and the worst criticism that can be leveled at any piece of writing (besides that it is boring) is that it is not truthful. (You must forgive my ranking untruthfulness as *second* among writing's worst characteristics, but a case can be made for the value of clever fiction over that of boring truth. Alfred North Whitehead, after all, insisted that "in the real world it is more important that a proposition be interesting than that it be true. "The importance of truth," he said, "is that it adds to interest.") Some storytellers tell the truth by recording history, others by rewriting it, and some by inventing it. To wonder which approach a writer is using seems unnecessary, unless, of course, one is more interested in history than in truth. I'll be bold enough, then, to say that *all* these stories happened—I just don't always know to whom.

First Person Singular

> "Nine years ago, I surrendered. I walked into my first AA
> meeting and started learning how to live."

I recently received a letter from a stranger that began with those lines. Immediately I was smitten. The writer had grabbed me and made me want to read. The reason why is simple: he wrote in the first person and from the gut (a place a little lower than the heart and deeper).

Most of the pieces here also are written in the first person because people's voices are best heard, I believe, when they speak for themselves. Of course this style runs the risk of seeming to impose the author's voice on each of the characters. My goal,

however, is to allow them to retain their own voice; to step aside
and let you encounter directly the unique personality of each char-
acter in the words and tone of his or her own story.

How to Use the Book

Most of all, I think, this is a book for personal reflection, a
resource for spirituality and personal growth. As mentioned
above, it is a book that hopes to give you *space* in which to be
and feel; and a book that hopes to awaken memories—memories
of experiences of confusing grace and of your many encounters
with the God of disguises.

But the book hopes also to be a resource for ministry. The pieces
here could be used on retreats or evenings of reflection as reflection starters, discussion starters, or as pieces of input. They also
can be used in liturgical prayer experiences as a way of focusing
the community—this is especially true of the proclamations in the
Dreams of the Kingdom section.

A number of the stories might be grouped and presented as
performance pieces by several players in a program of entertain-
ment and prayer. In such a setting the monologue-stories would
be memorized and music, costumes and lighting could be used to
enhance the drama of the presentation.

A grouping of these materials that has been especially useful and
effective for my liturgical performing arts company, *The Anawim
Players*, has included:

>First, eight to twelve selections from the *Sparks* section;
>Second, one of the proclamations from the *Dreams of the
>Kingdom* section; and
>Third, four to eight monologues from the other sections of
>the book.

Often this has taken the shape of a ritual-prayer experience that
concluded with some kind of ritual action (water blessing, anoint-
ing, etc.) that involved the entire gathered community. Music and
dance can also be made integral parts of the presentation. We use
instrumental music "behind" the *Sparks* pieces. A refrain or verse
is sung by the assembly in between every two of these mini-
monologues. During the singing each of the two speakers lights a
candle. At the conclusion of the set of mini-monologues the
candles are distributed to members of the audience-assembly as
the song is sung by all.

The proclamation that follows is spoken chorally. That is, sometimes a line is spoken by one person, other times by two or more, or even by all the speakers. Sometimes one person starts a line and another finishes it. You can create your own orchestration by being sensitive to the cadence of the lines, vocal variety, and the need for emphasis and build. Instrumental music is also helpful behind the proclamation.

A dance might follow the proclamation, or perhaps a song for the assembly.

Your selection of six to eight stories should balance darker and lighter moods and present a variety of life-situations.

A bridge between the stories and the concluding ritual is necessary—perhaps a water blessing prayer and an invitation to the assembly to participate in the blessing.[8]

Thanks

I want to give special thanks to all the *Anawim Players* who over the years have brought these stories to life in Chicago and throughout the United States: Patrick and Patrice Wooldridge, Patti Seitz Baranovskis, Eileen Evans, Miguel Gonzalez, Tria Thompson, Don Jabstrebski, Shirley Moore and of course, Nancy Marcheschi—thank you for loving and living these characters.

I also owe special thanks to all those (besides the *Anawim Players*) who have helped me believe in this material and who pestered me enough to get it published: Sue Antoinette, Mary Prete, Kathy Heskin, Connie Geiss, Mary Corneille, Leo Bourneuf, Barbara Marszewski, Adele Thibadeau, Joe Roccosalvo, Virginia Thoennes (who unwittingly got me started writing material like this), and all the others who were kind enough to listen and speak words of encouragement along the way. Thank you.

I wish to thank, too, Stephen Titra for the faith, support and talent he contributed to this project; and my publisher, Bob Heyer, for the chance to make this all happen.

And, finally, I want to thank the Lady of Nazareth.

---

8. Permission to perform this material without payment of royalty is granted only to amateur groups who charge no admission for their presentation and who purchase copies of this text for each player—mechanical duplication is not permitted. Professional groups are reminded that this material is protected by copyright and permission to use must be obtained from the copyright holder.

Wheat & Weeds and the Wolf of Gubbio

Paschal Mysteries

A Church with true spirituality is a creative Church . . . To encounter other human beings in the rough and tumble of this world, to experience life in the midst of death, and to perceive meaning in the face of meaninglessness—this is spirituality.

Choan-Seng Song, *Third Eye Theology*

TABERNACLES

It happened fast.

A feeble-brained innocent,
    refugee from half-way spaces,
moving at the wrong time:
    the Bread raised high,
    the Cup engaged in mystery,
and he chooses this time to change his seat
from one church side to the other.
For a moment his head blocks the view
of bread yielding to miracle.
For a moment his face and the bread are one.
The words spoken over both.

Then hands shake, extending proper peace;
cheeks meet,
words wish a peace the world has never tasted.
He stares, like a dog offered too many bones at once,
and accepts only one hand's greeting.

Next comes procession to his first meal of the day
as faces clearly wonder if he understands what this is all about.
He takes the proffered piece of pita
    in this most post-Vatican assembly
and stops.
Momentarily thrown by this bread with pockets,
he's oh-so-gently reassured that it's quite alright to eat.
He takes
and green teeth masticate the Body of Christ.
Then he reaches for the syrupped goodness of the cup

  (*Just three sips after him I debate the wisdom of changing lines.*)

His puffed-cheek mouthful nearly drains the cup.

  (*I almost wish he had so I wouldn't need to tell myself I won't
  catch some disease.*)

And then

   (*I knew it!*)

he coughs
and sends forth a rosy mist
that sprays Divinity unto the floor.
A rainbow comes and goes in that unexpected spray
as gasps are quelled in forty throats.
He clamps his mouth with leaky hands
looking like a child
trying to keep a pricked balloon from bursting.
drinks the pink God from the floor.
Unslackened, the line moves on
and Divinity is trampled by shod feet
till pure white linen,
   —bleached and starched—
in fervent hands that won't permit impiety,
drinks the pink God from the floor.

In a corner he sits alone
in rapt humiliation.
When someone asks, "Are you O.K.?"
he quickly shows his palms and says,
"I didn't wipe them on my dirty pants, I didn't.
I rubbed them hard together, see?"
and he demonstrates, with insect frenzy, how he used friction
to evaporate the spilled God from his hands.

Oh, what a cunning God
who tests our faith
by hiding in green-teethed
tabernacles
to see how truly we believe
in the miracle of real presence.

A FINGER DOWN MY THROAT

They came to me.
In the cave of my self-pity they found me
and demanded an explanation.
Friends can do that, they said,
demand to know
why a life is in a tailspin;
why a heart puts on a jacket,
pulls the collar up,
and turns its back to weep.
Alright, I said,
I'll tell you.

I rained on them the story of my sorrow:
the Judas kiss
the twisted knife
the salt rubbed in
the lies, the lies.
I showed my hands still bleeding;
my forever wounded side.
I spoke of slander served with smiles
in china cups.

And when I'd told the tale of this most unkindest cut,
      shared all the hurt, and anger, and despair;
when there was nothing left to tell,
one looked at me with bear-trap eyes
and spoke a single word:
        A thunder-clapping
        face-slapping
        heart-massaging word
        of just three letters
          that somehow built a bridge
          between my hell and healing.
This embarrassing word,
      not dignified enough to be a noun or verb,
crawled over me slowly,
like an ant in my pants,

making me freeze and squirm.
Yes, with simple eyes that once
    (oh, more than once!)
had looked on Calvary,
he looked at me
and with that syllable he shamed and saved me.
For when I had said it all
and the bile was about to choke me,
he shrugged his shoulders
and stuck a saving finger down my throat
by simply asking,

"And . . .?"

"And ...?"

So Easy

She was weird

And she wasn't smart
God, she wasn't smart
She included a biography of General Ulysses S. Grant in her
report on World War II

She didn't wash much
her clothes neither
and she ate her own bugers

She was the koody-bug

For eight years she went to school at St. Dachau
at Sixteenth and Paulina
and we shoved her into the ovens of our cruelty
and she didn't even put up a fight

For eight years we didn't touch her and when we did it was only
by accident or if sister was looking and then you had to pass the
koodies on but if you couldn't then you made a gun out of your
forefinger and thumb and you sssss'd with your mouth and
sprayed the part of your body that touched her body

This is my body...

I don't know how she put up with it
she should of transferred schools
I don't know why she didn't

In eighth grade when everyone got autograph books

even I got one—not the kind everyone else got from the company
that sells them to kids in school who are going to graduate that
have the school's name printed on them but one from a discount
store it cost four fifty less than the ones from the company—
my brother bought it for me and I'll always love him for that

anyway,
nobody asked for her autograph and nobody wanted her autograph and nobody would sign her book and she had one of the
books from the company and she bought it with her own money

Take this and eat...

and I saw her standing there looking around for an autograph and
after Harriett Horkle
the substitute koody-bug
there was nobody else in line to sign her book
and she was walking around real weird like she always did with
her sweater over her shoulders
and her shoulders going back and forth like a washing machine
and she didn't ask anybody
but she was just standing looking around and her face didn't say
get me out of this oven
she was practically smiling for Christ's sake
and she never cried in eight years she never once cried and said
Let this cup pass
and she never bought a ticket for Neuremburg
and she just looked around and waited
and her whole body was a Maranatha
and she scratched her dandruff and looked around and she didn't
scream
or cry
or bleed all over us

This is the cup...

But when no one else was in Suzanne's line
I went up
and she stopped scratching and handed me her book
and I signed it
it wasn't even hard
it wasn't hard at all
I never sprayed the koodies off anyway

so I didn't mind signing it
it was no big deal

and then I gave her mine to sign and she did
"Congrajulashuns!"
and that was it it didn't change her life or anything she didn't go
off and become prom queen of her school
        it probably didn't do a thing at all for her

But me, well

Whatsoever you do...

when I think of that day
I remember stepping up to a bar
and her pouring me a tall glass of salvation

and it went down so easy

OF BELLS AND TORNADOES[1]

Sometimes God comes disguised as a tornado . . . Don't ask me why. God's always been a mystery to me. Now if it were up to me, God wouldn't wear disguises . . . Oh, the problems it can cause . . .

---

1. The history of American health-care ministry is distinguished by the contributions of countless religious women who, despite frequent opposition from those in power, responded to the urgent needs of God's people. Among them are the courageous women who founded what is now the Mayo clinic to care for victims of a Minnesota tornado, and the Sisters of the Holy Cross and Sisters of Mercy who in the 1800's braved contagious cholera epidemics only to be repaid with bells around their necks so others could be warned to stay clear of the contagion. It is to brave women like these that this piece is dedicated.

Voices:

> I: *No, you shouldn't even attempt it!*

> II: *It has never been done before.*

> III: *It's much too dangerous an area, especially for women.*

For those who don't see through the disguise it's no problem at all. But those who recognize God, even in the guise of a tornado . . . well, they're in for real trouble.

Voices:

> IV: *No, sister! You must start simply and humbly!*

> V: *Being over-ambitious is a sure road to failure.*

> VI: *There are projects more suited to your vocation and . . .* talents where you can *serve God and the church.*

Now that's because recognizing God usually leads to conversation, and after listening and talking to God you just might hear some marching orders, and decide you ought to follow them. *But,* what God asks you to do might not be what everybody *else* thinks you *ought* to be doing. And that's where the problems begin!

For example if those sisters in Minnesota hadn't recognized God in the tornado, they might not have built that Mayo hospital that everybody told them couldn't be built.

Voices:

> I: *You ought to remain a "helpmate" and* assist *in this endeavor. Work out of your convent and do what's practical* and realistic.

> II: *Don't undertake a grand task of your own. Particularly one you know next to nothing about!*

But when the voice of God comes roaring through your town, and when you recognize God in the faces of all the people who got knocked about by that powerful wind . . . well you just gotta go and do what you gotta do no matter who's telling you not to. Right?!?   [*Bell rings*]

Sometimes God comes disguised as a bell. Just listen. [*Bell*]

I always think of God when I hear bells. And I think that every bell that ever rings is rung by God. Listen. [*Bell*]

Everybody hears it ringing. But not everybody knows who's ringing it or why. [*Bell*]

Could be the Bell of Freedom. God's for freedom, no doubt about it. Sometimes I think of freedom when I hear bells. [*Bell*]

Could be a firebell. God sets lots of things on fire; hearts and tongues. Sometimes when I hear bells I think of . . . Pentecost. [*Bell*]

Could be a leper's bell. God hangs out with lepers, you know?!? Makes them ring bells to remind everybody that it's God walking through. Did it two thousand years ago. Did it two hundred years ago. Except then it was a cholera bell. Not much difference. You see when those Sisters in Montana came to town ringing their bells in front of them, they reminded everyone that God lives in cholera victims too.

And who knows, they might use the bell again for some new thing . . . like AIDS. But if they do, when I hear the bell, it'll just remind me that it's God passing through.

Well, it's a problem though, these disguises God takes on. They're so darned good, you'd never know it was God if you weren't really looking. But I guess it hasn't worked out so badly, huh? In spite of a lot of people saying . . .

Voices: [Here and below, several players can speak the Voices lines from offstage, or the solo performer can speak them all, in quick succession, as if "quoting."]

      I: *You're crazy!*

     II: *You're drunk!*

    III: *You're wrong!*

    IV: *You're presumptuous!*

      I: *You're not submissive!*

     II: *You're too young!*

    III: *Too old!*

    IV: *Too inexperienced!*

  ALL: *You'll never make it!*

Despite all that, a lot of people, women mostly, saw through the disguises, and heard bells ringing, and built some very special places where God can be recognized in broken bread . . .

Voices:

      I: *Broken bones.*

     II: *Awe-filled births.*

    III: *In dignified deaths.*

    IV: *In calmed fears.*

      I: *In shared anguish.*

Yeah, special, holy places where a disguised God walks and mends broken lives. Oh yeah, special, holy places that stretch across a land where the broken bell of freedom rings.

(*Bell . . . Bell . . . Bell . . .*)

A STORY OF GRACE

It had been my third death that day.

The first two were devastating. This one . . . impossible.

I listened as the child's father raged, raged, raged
against the darkness of his pain;
and watched the mother enter,
silently,
the tomb of her great grief.

I knew, suddenly, that I had to act or it would be too late.

I sat beside her, took her hand and cried for her.

And when she touched my tears and blessed herself,
as if with holy water,
I knew that I had robbed death once again.

THE MOST RADICAL THING

She told me she was fleeing political persecution. I didn't know if it was true or not. But we took her in.

I know it was a big risk . . . They'd started a major push to find illegals . . .

We found her a job. It didn't pay anything. To be honest, I could never do that kind of work myself. But it made her feel less dependent, less of a charity case. She paid us rent—$40 a month.

Then one day she didn't come home. We got frightened immediately. I can't honestly say who we were more frightened for . . . her or ourselves.

The worst part was we didn't know what to do. We couldn't call the police and report her missing. We felt completely helpless. Three women scared to death of doing something, AND of doing nothing. We held hands and prayed . . . a long time.

Then I got a sense of peace. I stopped worrying.

I'd said that I would never do anything more radical than shelter an illegal immigrant. But that night, as we held hands and prayed, and I let go of the fear . . . that was the most radical thing I've ever done.

His father's son

His daddy was a preacher and when his daddy died
well, he died too,
    or nearly:
a year in a hospital bed is close enough to rising from the dead,
the drunk driver spent less time waiting for the trial.

But his daddy's funeral was beautiful
and everyone cried
    except him, of course,
and everyone was there
    except him, of course,
    and his Mamma
she survived too,
    or nearly;
everyone said she'd never be the same if she came to,
so when she did, she wasn't.

He became his daddy right on schedule:
Made his sweetheart a preacher's wife
and was a model of the ministry
till one day he took everything with him
and left everything behind
and he never came back
not him.

Now he's a carpenter in Colorado
living through his long hair like a 60's Sampson
and he pounds nails something fierce.
he's free now, he says
as he rattles his chains,
free
to be
what
he
wants

and he doesn't have to be what he doesn't want
but he doesn't want to be what not being what he doesn't want
has made him
and he rattles his chains as he swings the hammer

If you weren't there, there was no funeral

And maybe someday he'll have driven enough nails
into that coffin
to seal it shut for good
and bury it proper
and go on.

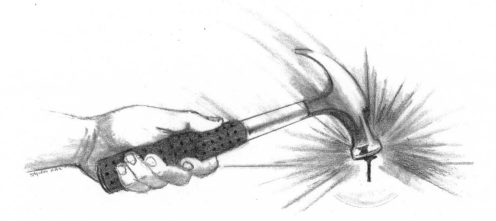

PRAYER OF RECOGNITION

I watched from the corner so they wouldn't see me. Steve was 87 years grumpy and had moved onto the floor when he was 84 years angry. Most of us kept our distance because he was one of those residents who could make you wonder if maybe you were in this just for the money after all. It was only 10:00 AM and he was on his fifth game of solitaire.

Joey, leading the pack of "holy clowns," had burst into the room without knocking, his clown face sporting a painted tear and an "I lost my front tooth just this morning in my waffle" smile.

Steve looked up from his cards and gave Joey a look that could have stopped a cyclone. They stared at each other a long time. When Joey launched himself at the bed, his right arm extended in greeting, Steve thrust out his right hand to defend himself. Their hands collided and snapped into a clasp: man and boy froze, staring intently into each other's eyes.

In the liturgy of that moment their eyes,
looking in the mirror of the other's face,
began a dance of recognition,

till the boy,
taught too well not to linger where he's not invited,
made a clean and sudden exit: stage right.

And the old man,
so close to unveiling his own gap-toothed smile,
returned to his solitary cards.

ALL I WANT FOR CHRISTMAS

I have a cousin, well, he's my wife's cousin, really; fought in Vietnam, came back really messed up—no direction, drugs, couldn't keep a job, trouble with the law, the whole bit.
One Christmas he came to our house for a party, really loaded as usual—booze *and* drugs—and one minute he's cracking jokes and the next minute he's sitting in my lap.

I felt real uncomfortable cause I didn't know what you say to a cousin who's three years *older* than you who's suddenly sitting in your lap. My kids thought it was real funny. So I pretend to be Santa Claus and I say, "What would you like for Christmas, little boy?"

Well, he doesn't hesitate for a second and out he comes with, "I want a Daddy just like you." And smack, he plants a kiss right on my cheek.

Crazy thing was, I knew he meant it. But what the hell could I say? His real father was right in the room. What do you say to a man who's asking for a father right in front of his father? It was the damndest thing!

But he changed the subject pretty quick. Started laughing, you know, cracking jokes. Like I said, he was loaded.

FATHER'S DAY

An old man in the park feeds the squirrels.
Unafraid, they nibble from his hands
the crumbs and nuts which are their daily bread.
Children and their mothers look on in fascination.
Young lovers resolve they'll do the same
when they grow old.
The evening news came once
and did a feature on the man who feeds the squirrels—
a model of gentle goodness
and kindness to the least.

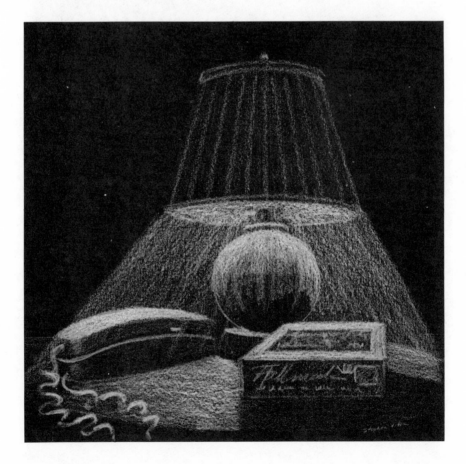

In Cleveland
Denver
and Detroit
two sisters and a brother live
who used to call him "Dad."
They don't know he feeds the squirrels;
don't know if he still feeds himself,
or if he's feeding worms.
And they don't care.

How could it be that a man who smiles at children,
who pours his life out for the squirrels,
and inspires romantic notions of old age
in those who are yet young—
how does it happen that such a man
owns a phone he never uses
and a box of Hallmarks all unsent?

STILL LOOKING

I'm not a sentimental guy. Just about anybody could tell you that.
Objectively speaking the kid was cute. I don't care who you are,
you had to give him that. Blond as the fuzz on a peach, smiling
like he was getting paid for it, and wearing a Cubs shirt that made
him look like a future all-star, for Pete's sake. He was five years
old and he should have been running through the sprinkler or chasing a damn squirrel, but there he was in the field-house grinning a
whole paycheck's worth. I was there to pick up my daughter—
who *was* chasing a squirrel—and before I could ask the supervisor
where she was, this kid walks up to me with that megawatt smile
and asks, "Are you my Daddy?"

So of course I laughed. Well, I mean it was a funny question.
He kept smiling and looking at me like he wanted an answer. So
I stopped laughing and I said, "Why, do I look like your dad?"

He looked at me for a couple of hours, I mean seconds—that
smile practically blinding me, for God's sake. Then he ran out to
the slide.

I guess it was the look on my face that brought the park supervisor over. She said his father had run off when the boy was just a
baby, so he doesn't know what his father looks like. She said he
asks lots of men that question.

I told my wife about the kid. I even told the guys at work—they
laughed and asked what ELSE I'd been doing on my bowling
nights. I told everybody I could. I thought maybe if I talked
about him enough I could get him out of my head. Didn't work.
I even dreamed about the kid: going up to strange men asking,
"Are you may daddy?" But a couple of minutes after I'd wake up
I'd forget all about the dream. And when my kids called me
"Daddy," I was just glad they knew who *their* father was.

Then one night I had that dream and *I* was the little kid looking
for his dad. I knew I was supposed to be the little blond boy
from the park, but at the same time I knew he was me. Even had
my beard. Five years old with a beard! And the kid kept asking
that question: "Are you my Daddy?"

That dream I didn't forget. In fact, I thought about it for a long
time. It's funny, when I first met that little boy in the park, I
started wishing I could do something for them. . . you know, kids
looking for their daddy. But after that dream, I started wishing
somebody could do something for us . . . you know, kids looking
for our daddy.

THE LAZARUS WALL

Between the Founding Father's obelisk
and the Emancipator's temple
they've built a wall
a "V" of marble
that reaches out like two black arms
to embrace the walking wounded
the unburied dead
who come as pilgrims to a pilgrim wall
a wall of names
the wailing wall
an American wall
in the American city.

They come
the sons and fathers
of the lost sons and fathers
    who left parents orphaned
    and children
        asking
          "Why."

They come
the wives and lovers
and the survivors
some to remember
some to erase
what cannot be erased.

They come
singing songs of loss
and endless hurt
of holes unfilled and wounds unhealed
of souls sliced with knives that look like telegrams
    and say how sorry,
    and how sad,
    how tragic and how valiant,
    how noble,
    and how wasted,
    and how dead!

Here at the wall—
   the pilgrim wall
   that says
   it's not over—
the names speak life and conjure images
of walking, laughing men
who once were boys who played with guns
until the guns played with the boys.

And now there's just the wall
a tombstone wall
above a grave that holds memories
      and guilt
          arrogance
             and ignorance
and wisdom birthed by pain;
a pilgrim stone
that visits cities to remind them of their loss
a stone so shiny that you see yourself when you read the names
    and it's so right
      that you see yourself when you read the names
      the names of the dead.

And you hope some morning you'll arrive to find the stone
    rolled away
and someone dressed in white asking why you come here
    to seek the living.
But that won't happen
where a tombstone wall marks a mammoth grave
that won't give up its contents.

So you give up your tears
and join the many
who come not to raise the dead
but to be buried with them
   (four days at least)
hoping
that in the darkness of the tomb
   (where surely there's a stench)
you will hear a voice
      a minstrel's voice

      who turns tear-drops into music
      who knew the walking wounded
      and feared the silent tomb
      who wept over city walls
      and yearned to gather with hen-like wings

daring in the darkness
to hope
that he's the one who listens
as you stand before the wall
who takes your tears and trains them to be music
and who will sing
      as he did once
            (when sisters wondered where he was)
a song that cannot be ignored
that brings the living
back to life
with just two words . . .

... Come Forth!

Laments

---

*The task of prophetic ministry is . . . criticism
and energizing. . . . Real criticism begins in
the capacity to grieve because that is the most
visceral announcement that things are not
right. . . . Bringing hurt to public expression
is an important first step in the dismantling
criticism that permits a new reality.*
Walter Brueggemann, *The Prophetic Imagination*

*F*OOT *IN THE MOUTH*

Why does it seem that my foot feels as much at home in my mouth as it does in my shoe!?! I always think I'm such a damned expert. Give me an issue and I've got an opinion.

Feminism? O.K.!

Two friends were talking about how some women are refusing to baptize their daughters because they don't want to initiate them into a church which "won't give them full personhood. Women are leaving the Church," they said, "what other choice do we have?"

"That's the problem," I said, "everyone wants to demand justice into existence, and if it doesn't happen fast enough they take their marbles and go! But you can't demand justice into existence. You have to birth it. Don't you see?!? When you demand justice you create a child that's orphaned before it's even born, and it enters a hostile world where there's no one to nurture and protect it. Justice can't survive in that kind of environment—it's too fragile. Look at Iran, look at Cuba. NEW boss, same as the OLD boss.

"Justice," I said, "has to be birthed. And that means fathering and mothering it into existence. Fathering it by creating a safe space, a welcoming environment where it will grow and thrive. Mothering it by being willing to endure the labor pains of its birth. That's what the great women and men with the big "S" little "t" in front of their names have always done. They didn't quit when the going got tough . . . they stuck around, and had a baby!

"Of course there's lots wrong with the church and it's GOT to change! But we've got to birth them changes Miss Scarlet, and don't you tell me you don't know nothin' about birthing babies!"

Well, that's what I said, and I felt pretty darned proud of myself, too! I'd never stood up to a feminist before, only to my husband, and believe me he's no feminist.

Then I went home . . . and my foot grew three sizes right inside my mouth. I looked at my own life and saw all the situations in which I demand justice. Like the man at work who's made it his life's ambition to attend my funeral before I'm 37. How many times have I just plain wanted him FIRED! No more talking, no more compromising, no more patience! He resents me, he's jealous of me, he's sick in the head . . . get him out, out, OUT! When it comes to him I don't want to know nothing about birthin'.

That's the night I started chewing. I'm working my way through that great big foot one toe at a time. And I decided I'd better not talk about 'birthin' or anything like that, till I've at least worked my way down to the heel. How could I? . . . I'm too busy . . . chewing!

LAMENT PSALM I

Never again
we say it
we pray it
we slice our veins and ooze it from our bodies

never again, oh God,
never again

but everyday
every damn day, oh God—
are you deaf
don't you see it
when a man takes a sweat-sock
and chokes the life of his live-in lover
and won't stop there
but wraps that cotton noose around her children's necks
      —seven and one year old for God's sake!
and proudly sends them to oblivion

I hear the horror
      —too late to change the station
and my body jerks
my mind searches for an answer
and it's ever again
ever again
the ugliness and pain
the jerking and the searching and the horror
everyday

my body moans a foreign word
my tears spell it on the table
come
damn it
come now
I dare you
come to the horror
come to the waste

come to the chopped up lives that mock your so-called goodness
come
not like the first time to be swallowed up, digested, and spit out
    what good was that?
    they say that one time was enough—the world was changed
but still the monster comes with fangs and claws
and nets of darkness
and everyday life is taken
everyday someone grieves
someone collapses in despair
everyday
and you sit around waiting for what
enough moaning and enough tears
to spell the word so big that even you can't miss it
well here it is
written in blood
and sweat from dirty socks
written with a jerky hand that just turned off the radio
here it is written so the king of England won't need glasses

Maranatha

o.k.
is that good enough
come

I *HEAR YOU*

I hear you.
In the cheers and shouts of football fans I hear you.
Riding El's and taking tests I hear you.

Oh nagging, prying, relentless God
I hear your shepherd voice calling me
out of the fold.
Can't you just accept that I long to be
just like the rest of them?

Why must you haunt me,
jab me,
grab me by the neck
and turn me toward Jerusalem?

Why make a fool of me?
Don't you know that hearing voices isn't fashionable?
Stop whispering sweet nothings in my ear.
I'm not one to long for consummation in a bonfire!

The earplugs of noisy crowds and raucous fun
of bars and bands and beers
don't work.
You still barge in and make a noise much louder than the rest.

I hear you.
And so I turn my head while others simply sit
and do my salmon run
upstream
against the flow of everything I know and understand
hoping they won't notice or think me strange
for doing cartwheels at funerals
or praying with basketball beads.

Will I always be a jack-in-the-box cranked by an invisible hand,
a clown with mis-matched socks
and too-big shoes
just because wax won't build up in my ears
and I can hear you?

HIS WAY

Connie Chung, looking gorgeous and sounding like a man who didn't want to be mistaken for a woman, was substituting for Dan Rather, and his wife was late again—which was not uncommon, though less common now since he put his foot down, right on the dog's tail, which was her dog and which she said he did on purpose just to spite her, and which, though he would never admit it to her, maybe he did.

The news was typically depressing—hostages, airline crashes, and sports heroes turned defendants—so he listened in the way that kept him sanguine despite it all, with a drink in his hand and his favorite music playing: Sinatra singing *"My Way."*

During the commercials, which he muted—an action that brought him no small satisfaction—he thought of what he would say when his wife finally came home. He rehearsed lines stuffed with anger and sarcasm, and he came up with some zingers, he thought; a recipe for vengeance he could market.

When his wife arrived, he pretended not to notice, mixed another drink, turned up the volume on the stereo, and sat, silent, before the moving pictures on the screen.

PRAYER OF A NURSE ON BREAK

I'm going to quit my job.
Today.
That's it . . . I mean it!
Why do I need to know that two young brothers died
within four days of one another,
teen-age victims of the demon cancer?
Why should I enter the E R to learn a gun erased another life
—and she not yet used to being called "Mommy—"
her husband's tears watering the fertile ground of my own grief.
Do I need the face of AIDS to pry open my sleepy eyes
and flush them with a saline wash?
Must I drink tears from my own coffee cup
and read Good Friday headlines on each break?

It's more than I can take, these daily doses of human misery
These horror stories of babies abandoned, burned, abused. . .
Of parents and children finding new-bloomed love
only in time to decorate the funeral home and grave.
I am not that burdened traveller triple-falling up the hill
with a resurrection carrot at his nose.
No Simon lifts the weight from my bruised shoulders.
My knees wont spring rabbit-like for the carrot goal.

I sit with luke-warm coffee,
and hot anger welling up in my eyes,
my fingers smudged with the same blood-ink that wrote
yesterday's woes
and will write tomorrow's!

When you were hoisted on the hill and looked out upon the ages
and heard the echoes of your pain bouncing back
from every sick bed, every ghetto
didn't you despair and cry the prayer of the forsaken?

Can't I burn this uniform then,
and seek a warm womb of refuge
from the pain that cuts like a plow through the fields of my life?
Can't I crawl into a tomb as dark as yours
and shut my eyes to stop the torrent-tears that flood the ground?

But every time I do
I find you in the tomb
        lying somewhere between sleep and waking
body gripped by an overwhelming force
ready,
seed-like,
to thrust a courageous shoot
through the pain-tilled ground.

GOOD SONGS

There aren't any good songs anymore.
Was a time when songs asked big questions.
You know?
"Where have all the flowers gone?"
"How many roads must a man walk down. . .
    before they call him a man?"
Don't know if anybody ever figured out the answers,
but damn!
they were good questions.

LAMENT PSALM II

Where is the god of blood and guts?
    the god of orgasms?
Who do I call when my anger boils
        and when I need to rage?
Where have you put the god of passion,
    the seducing god,
        the god of sexual threat?

Is there no god of strength,
        and rippling muscles?
What happened to the god of flint and fireworks;
    the god of hard knocks
        and hard feelings?

What happened to the god who thunders,
    the god who belches lava?
When did god stop throwing hammers,
    and lightning bolts,
        and tantrums?

Does god sing only folk songs
        and shun the get-down blues?
Is there no god of rock-and-roll,
    who snaps his fingers,
        pounds the drums
            and plays air-guitar with the band?

Did god quit downing shots and beer
    and start sipping Perrier and white wine?
When did god hang up his jock-strap
    and go have a vasectomy?

I need a god of fire,
    a god of strong emotions,
        a god who gets as mad as I do,
who gets a hard-on now and then.

And if you think that's blasphemy,
then you just pray to your god

and I'll keep looking.

*P*RAYER OF THE STREETLIGHT

Some people are comets, God.
They make a grand entrance
and light up the sky with a brilliant glow.
They might come round only every seventy-five years or so,
but when they do the whole world comes out to watch;
and they leave a tail behind them that glows, glows, glows . . .
and then they're gone.
Wow!

I'm just a street lamp, God.
My glow isn't so bright.
I never make an entrance.
I'm just there.
No fanfare. No hoopla.
I'm just there.

Sometimes
someone stops and leans against me just to rest a bit,
or to read directions they wrote on some piece of paper they pull
        from their pocket.
Once in a while I burn out
and people cuss me
and call the city to complain.
The scary streets are a bit less scary when I'm there,
and people stumble less when I'm around.
But it feels so small what I do,
compared to those comets.
People wait for them.
They study them.
No one studies me.
Comets never seem to burn out
and no one calls the city on them.

I . . . I long to be a comet sometimes.
To blaze a trail across the sky with the whole world looking on
and taking pictures to show their grandchildren.

When comets land they leave big footprints
and everyone knows where they've been;
and sometimes they put markers there so no one will forget.
People only notice me when they're in trouble:
        when it gets too dark to see what they're doing
        or too scary to walk alone.
I don't light up the sky,
only a little corner of the earth.
So little, so small . . .
It would be great to be a comet—
to make a splash!

But once
a child told me,
a young child just a fraction of my age . . .
    (Praised be you, Lord of heaven and earth,
    for what you've kept hidden from the learned and clever. . . !)
. . . the child told me
that splashes dry up . . .
and comets go away.

Small comfort, God, that at least I'm there.

But, God, at least I'm there.

PRAYER OF THE COMET

Some people, God, are streetlights.
Burning steady day after day.
Reliable.
Predictable.
Consistent.

I'm a proud comet
blazing, dazzling, illuminating the sky,
for just a day or two,
and then
I'm gone.
I don't know how to be there everyday.
You gave me legs,
and marching orders,
and ears deaf to the word
"Halt!"

People make a doctor's office sound as I go by
and open their mouths wide . . . "aaah!"
So what?!?

People's lives are on the earth.
Only dreamers watch the sky,
and dreamers are asleep living fantasy not life.
Streetlamps are where the living is.
They light up important places:
Streets
        where children play and lovers meet,
        where commuters wait for buses that go home,
        where painted women wait for farm boys,
        where hands are cuffed and backs are stabbed,
        where winos beg and buddies spare a dime.
Under those lights wheat and weeds grow up together
and even when you can't tell them apart
at least you know that they're alive.
I roam a sterile vacuum
with galaxies of stars that don't breathe or bleed,
and most of them shine twice as bright as I.
I might look good,
but only on those rare occassions when I come close enough,
and the lights are fixed just right,
to make my complexion glow,
but still stay far enough away
so the pock-marks on my face don't show.
I come just close enough to see what I'm missing
but not close enough for them to see who I really am.

It must be great to be a street lamp
knowing those who walk by
—no need to impress—
giving them a place to rest on their way
or lighting their path home.

I long to be planted sometimes.
Rooted.
Where people can know where to find me.
Streetlamps get their power from somewhere else—
they know that,
everybody knows that.
When they light up,
people know who's light they're shining.
And streetlights know they have to stay plugged in
or they go out.

Comets don't have to be plugged in.
Poeple think we make our own light.
And sometimes I think the only thing my light lights up
is me.
I streak across the sky,
but all I'm saying is "Here I am. . . here I am. . . here I am!
Look. . . listen. . . follow!"
So what?!?
What good is it to live up where only dreamers look?

But yesterday,
when I was feeling down
and thinking stars are worthless next to streetlights,
a child reminded me that once
three men followed a star . . .

and found you.

Breakthroughs

Madness need not be all breakdown. It may also be breakthrough.

Ronald David Laing, *The Politics of Experience*

*H*IS FAVORITE SONG

I don't have a favorite song.
Some people do.
"What's your favorite song?" you ask,
and they tell you right away.

I wish I had one.
But every time I hear one of the great songs,
the old songs,
THAT'S my favorite song!
Sometimes they play a string of golden oldies on the radio
and each one enters my veins and rushes through my bloodstream
and sings me
moves me
snaps my fingers and claps my hands
—usually I'm in my car putting on a mime show for the driver
next to me—
but as I'm listening to that tune
it's the only song in the world
and the only one I want to hear.

Then
—when it's finished and the next song begins—
God, I don't believe it!
but THAT'S the only song in the world.
My body bounces
my voice swells
and the whole world shrinks.
And it's just me and the music
and the joy.
And the past bursts into pieces
that land inside my car
and they move to the rhythm of the music
leading the song
and following it.
And the song is just so good that no one could have written it
unless they stole fire from Olympus
and the flames leapt onto the page and picked places on the staff.

And the song is never going to end
because it's too darn good to end
and it's miracle and magic . . .
till it stops.

      And
          as I'm
              falling
                    off
                        the mountain
          another song catches me
          and holds me in its arms

and it starts all over again
because now this, THIS is the only song in the world.
Really!

And one day I had a vision:

Jesus was driving a car
and each person was a song
—the only song in the world—
And he went nuts with each new melody
cause that one,
      and that one,
          and that one

was the only one
in the world.

YOU MAY BE RIGHT

I met a man who said,
"Christians are people who suck lemons."
"You may be right," I said.

But in the morning,
when the sun was shining and the moon was put to bed,
I looked at him and said,
"Christians, really,
are people who suspect
that on the third day
what rolled the stone away from the entrance
was a sudden burst of laughter
from inside the tomb."

stephen fitz

SISTERS[1]

MARY and MARTHA (*Alternating*):
I've kept a secret for many years.
> *There's a secret I've kept for many years.*
It was my sister who loved him best!
> *It was my sister who loved him best!*
She is so different from myself.
> *We're so different, the two of us.*
She lived for Jesus; he was her life.
> *Jesus was her whole life.*

---

1. This piece is meant to be presented by two women sitting side-by-side looking out, never at each other. Each is remembering, so she gazes off into the distance in order to "see" the scenes and characters she describes. It's important that the two establish a seamless rhythm, as if each were the only speaker; we should never feel that one is waiting for the other before she can continue her thought. Though for the most part each is pursuing her own train of thought, occasionally the two converge and we have the effect of one finishing the other's sentence. When alternating, they speak in the order they are listed.

Everything Martha did, she did for him.

Mary did everything for him.

Nothing was more important.

Nothing was more important to her.

She would drop everything when he came, and he knew it.

When he came, Mary dropped everything.

Martha always did what she did best, and Jesus loved her for it.

Mary did what she did best, and Jesus loved her for it.

She wished she could be like me, really, because she thought he loved me better.

She really thought he loved me better.

But I knew that wasn't so.

I knew that wasn't true.

He loved her simplicity.

He loved . . . her simplicity.

And when he came, she always seemed to know just what to do.

When he came, she knew just what to do.

MARY (*Standing*):
She headed for the kitchen. Martha always knew he was coming long before he reached the house. "The rabbi's coming," she'd announce. I'd look through the window and there he'd be walking toward the door, and Martha already in the kitchen preparing something for him . . . and for the many who came with him. She was alive in that kitchen preparing food for him. She sang then. My mute sister, singing! I envied the joy that work brought her. There's no doubt she loved him, and every time she saw him she knew precisely what to do. (*She sits*)

MARTHA (*Standing*):
He'd come in and she'd sit down. Simple. Oh, how he talked and how she listened. Mary heard nothing else when Jesus spoke. I'd have to shake her to get her to come into the kitchen to finish preparations. But I soon gave up trying. There was such joy on her face as she listened, as if a world opened up and beckoned her in. I sometimes thought she had stopped breathing as she watched him, and I longed to see what her eyes could see. I know she loved him, and every time she saw him she knew *exactly* what to do. (*She sits*)

MARTHA and MARY (*Alternating*):
But I just did what came naturally.
  What I did just came naturally.
I wanted to be like my sister,
  I wanted to be like Martha.
but Jesus' presence was so powerful it crippled parts of me;
  Sometimes his presence crippled me,
so I just did what I knew how to do.
  So I did what I knew how to do.
It was the only way I could breathe.
  It was such an effort breathing in his presence.
Like when you've climbed a mountain:
  The air is different.
He had the same effect as wine;
  He affected me like strong wine

making me weak and warm at the same time.
He could make me weak and warm at one time.
(*Both together:*)
At least, that's what he did for me. But perhaps for my sister it was different.

MARTHA:
She became beautiful when he was near; and happy. A light went on inside her eyes. Sometimes I'd notice people watching *her* when Jesus spoke, as if his presence was too much for them, and they could only bear to watch him in a mirror. But she was more than a mirror, my sister. Mary was a portrait, an interpretation of who he was. I'd almost say a self-portrait of Jesus, for it was as if he *used* her face to reveal parts of himself. And she was glad to be his canvas. If I've ever seen pure joy, it was in my sister's face when she was with him.

MARY:
Her face changed in his presence. It softened and shone. He gave her a sense of who she was, a sense of purpose. She didn't hesitate, or question, or need anyone's approval. People sometimes used her as a filter of his words. Often they would rise in the middle of his speaking to join her in the kitchen. "What did he mean by that," they'd ask. For though she worked, they knew Martha never missed a word he said. She would explain, then shoo them back to listen for themselves, and continue her kitchen contemplation. When she was near him, Martha was the definition of pure happiness.

MARY and MARTHA (*Alternating*):
It seems ironic that this man who brought the best out of my sister, made me turn weak and helpless in his presence.
How could this man who drew the best out of my sister make me so weak and helpless?
I only did what I could do, and *had* to do. Nothing more.
I only did what I had to do in front of him. No more.
Yet that was always enough for him.

For him, that was enough.
I don't know why he was so gentle with me.
He was so very gentle.
(*Both together:*)
But his acceptance is what I remember best.

MARTHA and MARY (*Alternating*):
It branded me and made me his forever!
He branded me forever!
And though I think my sister loved him more,
though my sister loved him more
somehow I know that for his part
for his part
the love he felt for me
was no less
than what he felt
(*Both together:*)
for her.

Stephen Titra

EPIPHANY

One day I stood in the rain waiting for the rainbow.
The rain flung itself at me,
but I didn't budge.
It stung my face and chilled my courage,
but I stood firm.
It made the thunder shout its threats
and with the lightening stabbed my eyes.

I didn't move.
I waited for the rainbow.
The wind conspired with the rain and both tried to knock me
down.
But my eyes were fixed. My focus didn't waver.
I knew that God was in the rainbow.
So I waited.

And then the rainbow came.
At last, I gasped,
and reached out arms to grasp the living God . . .
and found there was no rainbow.
It's a trick!
A masterful illusion.
A rainbow is just color
discovered in the rain.

And who would have thought that God is just the same,
a master of illusion,
who all these years was waiting,
not to be rainbowed,
but to be recognized
in the rain
that flung and stung and thundered in my face.

WHEAT AND WEEDS AND THE WOLF OF GUBBIO[1]

Today's Gospel was the Parable of the Wheat among the Weeds. I think the priest preached a good sermon on it, but I missed it. As soon as the Gospel ended, I started thinking about my Dad. All his life my father was a fanatic about two things: horror movies and a weed-free lawn.

The lawn satisfied his need to keep his world under control. Dogs didn't dare leave souvenirs on our lawn. Falling leaves knew better than to land in our yard, and weeds, well let's just say any weed foolish enough to enter our yard soon learned the meaning of "kamikaze mission." He could spot a dandelion from the breakfast table and be out the door and back again, with a satisfied grin on his face, before my mother could pour him a fresh cup of coffee.

His other passion was horror movies, and his particular favorites were movies about werewolves. We saw them all, my dad and I, from Lon Chaney to Michael J. Fox, with my father jabbing me in the ribs to punctuate all the most exciting parts.

Weeds and werewolves. Hated one and loved the other.

As he grew older he started sprouting—now don't get grossed out—ear and nose hair. It traumatized him! Hair growing at will in places where he didn't want it. He went after it with a vengeance, despite my mother's insisting it was sexy. I'd see him in front of the mirror snipping hair and hear him mumbling something about "These damn weeds." His fanatic efforts to be in

---

1. The *Fioretti*, or Little Flowers of St. Francis, is a collection of stories and fables about the great saint of Assisi. Among them is a the apocryphal tale of the Wolf of Gubbio. When a terrible wolf threatened their village, the citizens of Gubbio turned to Francis for help. Francis miraculously tamed the wolf and, in exchange for his docility, the townspeople agreed to feed the wolf daily. Soon the wolf became a much beloved member of the community—so much so, in fact, that when he finally died, the entire village mourned the death of "Friar" Wolf.

control, and to protect his lawn and his own body from unwanted growth made it all the harder to understand his fascination with werewolves. I mean, talk about loss of control and unwanted growth!

One night, as the credits of some old horror film were scrolling up our T.V. screen and I was feigning interest in the artists and technicians who had created this monstrous masterpiece, he assaulted my drooping eyes and nodding head with his best Lon Chaney imitation. Through bared teeth he hissed "Don't be frightened, my child, there is a wolf in each of us!" Then he sprang to his feet, howled a laugh, hit the T.V. switch and growled again, "A wolf deep down inside us all!" And he held his sides to contain his laughter. I laughed politely, but later I thought hard about his words. I guess I sensed a subconscious struggle in my Dad, some deep down approach-avoidance conflict, which expressed itself in his twin passion for weeds and wolves.

I inherited my father's dislike for weeds, but his passion for wolves eluded me. *Little Red Riding Hood, The Three Pigs*, and my sister's first attempts at dating taught me wolves weren't to be trusted.

Then I read about "Francis and the Wolf of Gubbio." And my father came leaping toward me from those pages. It's true the Parable of the Wheat and Weeds got lost on my Dad—he never saw the sense of letting weeds grow anywhere! But another part of him sensed that each of us is weed as well as wheat—only, for him, weeds came dressed in *wolves* clothing. The violent, uncontrollable parts of my Dad began to breathe and growl right along with Lon Chaney and every other man-to-wolf transmutation he witnessed on the screen. But that screen was his silver bullet, keeping at bay the frightening reality he sensed within himself. And maybe my dad spent so much time weeding the yard because he sensed, after all, that the wolf-weed in his heart was one of those which had to be allowed to grow along with the wheat.

It's been a long road for me since making that realization about my Dad; since reading the story of Francis and being convicted by his willingness to face that wolf, alone and unprotected, without the benefit of any "silver bullet."

Francis knew what my dad knew about what lives "deep down inside us all;" but he did what my Dad could never do. He stood helpless and vulnerable before the terrifying power of that renegade wolf. More than that, he recognized the wolf as brother, and he loved him. Francis knew that if he couldn't love that wolf, he couldn't love himself. No doubt Francis' own heart had sometimes filled with hurt and lupine anger. But he had learned that fear, denial and retaliation don't purge the heart of unwanted passions; though love and understanding might.

Francis' courage fed my own. And I have played the monk to the four-footed citizen of Gubbio in *my* soul; played mediator between him and the two-footed Gubbians in my life—those frightened citizens who have hurt and scarred me with their misunderstandings and their fears . . . and whom I've hurt.

Meeting Francis and his wolf has made it easier to remember that all the wolves I meet are just poor creatures like myself whose claws and fangs are no sharper than my own.

Now . . .
I pull fewer weeds, and watch more horror movies.
And I think my Dad would probably approve.

*B*UT THE TEENS KEPT COMING

For three years I watched him stick pins into her like she was some voodoo pin-cushion. Annie was my cousin, and all she wanted was to hold a teenage Bible study. After all, the kids had come to her. She'd get up early in the morning—before breakfast dishes, packing off the kids, and phone calls—to do her "homework." She read Scripture, and she read books about Scripture, and she prepared her lesson plans. Middle-classed, middle-aged and nowhere *near* the middle of the music or fashion scene. But the teens kept coming.

The group outgrew her living room, so she turned up at the rectory door.

"No, you cannot use the church basement for a Bible study. No one should teach scripture but a priest."

"But the kids want a Bible study. I just assumed you wouldn't mind . . ."

"But I do mind," he said. "Besides, the only ministry you can do with teens is social. Take them bowling."

But the teens kept coming; so the next couple of years got tough. Annie took a Scripture course and went through Lay Ministry Training. Her credentials were starting to look good. So the living room Bible study was "officially" banned. But the teens kept coming.

So the rumors started.

"Wasn't it a bit unnatural for Annie's eldest to enjoy his mother's company quite so much?"

But the teens kept coming. Petitions; letters from parents; parish meetings . . . and still no room at the inn.

Then Annie's mother died. And that's when I became involved. He came to concelebrate the funeral Mass. I'd prepared the liturgy and knew his presence would upset my cousin: Annie didn't need his intrusion on the day she buried her mother. So I made a whip of words and sought to drive him from the temple.

"Were you invited to concelebrate?" I asked.

"No, I just assumed . . ."

"Please, don't assume," I said.

He was never so insulted in his life. The alb was back on its hanger before I could run out to meet the hearse. As she emerged, I told Annie *he* was here, but leaving.

She found him . . . and he stayed.

I got mad and played Judas to her Jesus. "What a waste!" I said. "That kind of deference should be saved for people who deserve it. Don't pour out your ointment on a stinking bum!"

She was silent. But in that day's Gospel I heard my rebuttal: "Wherever the good news is proclaimed what she has done will be spoken of as her memorial."

Those words stung me with momentary guilt. But later, at the kiss of peace, Annie held me tightly as we hugged and whispered "Thank you" in my ear. And when my eyes met hers, her tears and grateful smile reminded me that we remember both the one who poured the ointment, *and* the one who tried to cleanse the temple.

*F*OR THE CHURCH

It was one of those phone calls in which you can hear the thunder of the gathering storm, but you tell yourself, "It was just some traffic noise or fireworks."

I'd already signed the contract. So what if the man who hired me was leaving and a new pastor would be my boss. Maybe he'd be even better to work for! Yeah, like the time I went through the red light doing 50, and hoped the flashing lights behind me were a tow truck!

Well, he was a racist. That's as kind as I can get. The parish was black and Puerto Rican. He was as pearly white as the handle on a revolver. And he could fire just as well. But when he fired the parish secretary, an African-American woman who'd been in the job for years, he used up his last bullet.

"You people are all alike," he said, "just a bunch of bastards!"

I was standing right there and had to duck to avoid the ricochet.

I told her to get a lawyer and made sure I got subpoened (my religious vows wouldn't let me volunteer a testimony).

We won in the county and state courts. But some low-down people in high places kept reloading his gun . . . and it kept on.

When we won in federal court it finally stopped.

Someone asked me if I had felt like a traitor—I think "Judas" was the word—for testifying against the Church.

I don't think he saw the tears in my eyes as I explained that my testimony had been *for* the Church.

PRAYER OF A COMPANION

I was sick. Sicker than I'd ever been before.

I was afraid.
I'd never really thought about dying. Now, I couldn't stop thinking about it.

This nurse kept coming in and telling me jokes.
Awful jokes, mostly.
But she laughed so hard every time she told one . . . I started
laughing with her.

The day they released me, I bought a box of candy
and gave it to her.

She told me, then, that she has cancer, too.
And we both laughed.

WORKING ON A DAY WHEN I SHOULD HAVE BEEN OUT PLAYING

A Spring sound penetrates my study
through a window opened just a crack
The voice of a child
calling her mother to ecstasy:

"Mommy! Mommy! Mommy!"

She, engaged in adult conversation,

"Mommy, Mommy!"

glimpsed, but didn't see, the explosion of joy

"I have a stick, Mommy, I have a stick!"

that turned the child's face into a monstrance

"I have a stick, Mommy!"

as she exalted in the find that made her the equal of her brother
who carried a limb as long as his arm and thicker.

"Mommy,"

she said, holding up a twig the size of her finger,

"I have a stick, I have a stick!"

PRAYER OF A HOSPITAL BILLING CLERK

Miracles? You want to know about miracles?!?
Well, I can tell you about miracles!

Did you know that every day in this building blind people are
made to see?
Yeah, you heard me right!

And the deaf begin to hear.
No, you don't need a hearing aid. That's what I said!

AND . . . lepers are made clean.
Exaggerating?!?
You talk to a kid with a bad case of acne and you *see* if she
doesn't feel like a leper.

AND the dead are raised to life.
So what if they were dead for only ten minutes—or five minutes—
or two! They'd still be dead if it wasn't for us!

Now if that's not reason enough to throw a party, then I don't
know what is! So if you feel like celebrating, come on in.

What do I do here?
I send out the bills.

Yeah, can you believe it, I put a price-tag on miracles.

Yeah, I know Jesus didn't do that.
But what he did do was to say, "Greater things than I have done,
you will do."
Now I'm not sure he had hospitals in mind whe he said that.
But if you don't think of hospitals, and medical centers, and nursing homes when you hear those words, then . . . you can't come
to the party.

But if you realize that miracles do happen here everyday;
then here's a balloon, a noisemaker, and an invitation!
Now on the count of three . . .
start celebrating!

Sparks

Thou waitest for the spark from heaven: and we
Light half-believers of our casual creed,
Who never deeply felt, nor clearly willed . . .
Who hesitate and falter life away,
And lose tomorrow the ground won today—
Ah! do not we, wanderer! await it too?

Matthew Arnold, *The Scholar Gypsy*

A great flame follows a little spark.

Dante Alighieri, *The Divine Comedy*

83

LOST CONTROL

Sometimes I feel like I've completely lost control.
I don't know why I do the things I do.
I don't know why I think the way I think.
I feel like I'm on a merry-go-round and the guy who runs it
'sgone on break . . .
and he's never coming back!

WHEN I WASN'T LOOKING

I used to be full of enthusiasm and . . . idealism.
I was going to change the world.
Then the world changed me.
It's like one day,
when I wasn't looking,
this other person slipped inside my body
and she just won't leave.

*F*UZZY *T.V.*

Maybe I'd have a better idea of where I'm going
if I had a better idea of where I've been.
It all goes by so fast.
It's like a fuzzy T.V.
and when you go to fix it . . .
the knob is missing.

SOME DAYS I

Some days I feel like a total failure.
The notes are sour,
the songs don't fit,
my choir thinks I'm a jerk
and I make the mistake of telling them what I think they are.

Then I go home,
dish out three scoops of my favorite ice cream,
and watch Jay & Letterman
as I pick up the paper and go through the want ads.
After writing down three or four phone numbers,
I go to bed and sleep.

Next morning, I throw away the numbers
and get back to work.

CIRCUS

When I was young and innocent,
life was a circus
because circuses are so exciting
and surprising.

When I was older and cynical,
life was a circus
because circuses are full of clowns.

Now that I'm older still, and tired
life is a circus
because the circus comes to town for not enough days,
and packs up and leaves
too soon,
too soon.

NEW JOB

Yesterday I signed my contract.
This morning my mother called.
She was excited about my new job at the parish.
I said I was too.
Then she asked about my salary.
I lied.
She said,
> Wasn't it wonderful that I could do the work I love
> and be appreciated, too!

*I*F YOU EXIST

I used to wonder if there really was a God.
"If you exist, God," I said, "show me your face."
And then one day my husband came home early from work,
skipped his bowling night,
and took us all out for dinner—
just because he remembered that it was a year ago that day
that we had to put my mother in the nursing home.

DISTANT MUSIC

When I was a kid life was a lullaby.
When I was a teen it became a rock concert.
After college I wasn't sure for a while,
but pretty soon golden oldies became my thing.
In mid-life I turned to classics;
and now, lullabies are sounding good again.

But every once in a while,
I think I hear a distant music.
I don't know where it comes from,
but I swear it's calling me.

CHILD'S TRUTH

I once heard a child misspeak a cliche.
Instead of "I can't believe my ears,"
she blurted,
"I can't believe my fears!"

And that struck me as remarkable wisdom.

DIFFERENT VERSES

My first week at Assumption I did three funerals,
a wedding,
and a baptism.
The baptism was fun.
The wedding was a circus.
And the funerals were tough.
But I couldn't stop thinking
that this crazy God had put me there
to show that baptisms,
funerals,
and weddings
are just different verses
of the same song.

NO MATTER WHAT

Sometimes the lump in my throat swells up so big
I want to tear it out.
But I decided,
the day my husband left me,
that no matter what,
I am not going to cry.

*H*EAVEN

If heaven was a theme park
and I was designing it
every attraction would be a restaurant
and there'd be no waiting
and you could sit as long as you like
and when you were done you wouldn't have to pay the check . . .
and you could start all over again!

*I*T'S FOR YOU

I was talking with some of my married friends
with teenage children
and someone said
"Isn't it funny how there used to be a time when,
if the phone rang,
it was for you;
and now the only time the phone rings and it's for you
is when someone calls to ask for money?"

GOOD TALKING

People talk better today than they ever did before.
You can go to the library and find a book
    on any topic under the sun,
and if you don't like that one
there's at least two or three others somebody else checked out.
Only thing I can't figure is why,
with all this good talking going on,
people aren't actin' any better than they ever did.

ALONE

I didn't use to mind being alone.
It was a sign of independence.
I was proud of it.
Now being alone is hard.
I get scared sometimes.
You see, I've done everything else there is to do alone.
But I can't help thinking
that that's not the way a person is supposed to die.

I DOUBT

When I see babies abused
and wives beaten,
women raped and men shot down,
I no longer doubt the existence of God.
I doubt, instead,
the existence
of human beings.

SOME DAYS II

some days i feel like i'm e.e. cummings
and everyone is trying to teach me how to capitalize!

WHAT THE HELL?

Something happened to hell.
Don't know what.
But it sure ain't what it used to be.
Used to be you didn't want to go there.
Used to be you could scare a grown man
   with talk of hellfire and brimstone.
No more.
Nope.
Nothing's "sure as hell" any more.
Hell ain't.
Seemed to me a mighty useful thing, hell was,
for setting fires *under* people:
      keeping 'em doing what they should
      instead of what they should'na.

Well, maybe they know best,
      them folks that cancelled hell.
But one thing I can't figure,
if there ain't no hell,
how come so many folks act like they went to school there?

Dreams of the Kingdom

Dreams are necessary to life.

Anais Nin, *Letter to her Mother*

Energizing is closely lined to hope. We are energized not by that which we already possess but by that which is promised and about to be given. . . . (One) energizing reality is a doxology in which the singers focus on (the) free One and in the act of the song appropriate the freedom of God as their own freedom. . . . Doxology is the last full act of human freedom and justice. Only where there is doxology can there be justice, for such songs transfigure fear into energy. . . . It is the vocation of the prophet to keep alive the ministry of imagination, to keep conjuring and proposing alternative futures to the single one the (dominant culture) wants to urge as the only thinkable one.

Walter Brueggemann, *The Prophetic Imagination*

In dreams begins responsibility.

William Butler Yeats, *Responsibilities*

SOMETIMES, A DREAMER[1]

In the beginning there was a dreamer.
Sometimes that's all it takes...
A dreamer
    of gentle heart and strong vision
        who knows when to act and when to pray
        who hears the cry of the poor and gladly sings their song
        who recognizes nailprints in needy hands and tired feet
        and who believes without placing hand in wounded side.
Sometimes one dreamer is enough to focus the vision of a nation.
And sometimes one dreamer's footsteps are so big
    that others follow and find their way along the path
Sometimes one dreamer sees so clearly
    that others become unafraid to look at things they never saw
    before

Sometimes one dreamer hears so well
    that others start moving to a music they never knew was
    playing
Sometimes one dreamer's faith is so clear
    that reality becomes larger than circumstances
    and no shock,
    no death or fire,
    no rejection or opposition,
    no misunderstanding or detraction
can rob their holy peace.

---

1. This proclamation was originally composed for a celebration of the 250th anniversary of the founding of the Grey Nuns. Written to honor the life and ministry of the community's foundress, Blessed Marguerite d'Youville, the piece was titled "Sometimes, a Woman." The piece is quite suitable for use to honor the foundress of a community. In such a case, the word "woman" would replace "dreamer" throughout the piece, pronouns would be adjusted accordingly, her name would replace "Jesus of Nazareth" [since it would then read: "In the beginning there was a woman . . .], and the litany of saints would be deleted. Years and numbers appropriate to the community's history would replace "two thousand years" and "millions of dedicated lives."

Sometimes a dreamer walks a smooth and level road
    that hovers above life's circumstances
and when the circumstances change or crumble
    the faith-path they walk remains stable and unshaken.
Sometimes . . . in hard times,
    always in hard times, never in easy,
such a dreamer appears
  and that time becomes
      God-time,
        Miracle-time
          Blessed and Sainted time
A dreamer comes
    who loses spouse
      and becomes refuge for the widowed;
    who watches children die,
      and becomes mother of the lost and abandoned
    who sees flames consume the work of years
      and becomes consumed with doing the will of God.
And those of us who long for miracles and saints
    look on and realize
      that no age is an age of saints
      until a single heart is born
      and, through its courage, makes it so.
And then,
  through the mystery and miracle of love,
one such heart becomes many:
Hands are multiplied
Promises are made
    and the hopeless find hope

the weary find rest
the homeless are sheltered
the hungry are fed
prisoners are visited
the dead are buried
a house in ruins is raised up
and God's Kingdom
        brick by painful, joyful brick,
becomes visible among us.
In the beginning there was a dreamer.
        Jesus of Nazareth,
who enflamed voices that continue to challenge,
Paul of Tarsus,[2]
        Augustine of Hippo,
Benedict and Scholastica,
        Francis and Clare,
Catherine of Sienna,
        Theresa of Avila,
Ignatius of Loyola,
        Joan of Arc,
Elizabeth Ann Seton,
        Thomas Merton
Dorothy Day,
        Oscar Romero,
Mother Theresa of Calcutta,
        Pope John XXIII
and in God's plan that's all it took
        to fashion a history that spans two thousand years,
        to engender a community that encompasses millions of dedicated
                lives,
        to establish centers of healing and learning,
        places of refuge and compassion,
        to inspire an uncompromising commitment to the poor,

---

2. Other names appropriate to the occasion and the celebrating community may
be substituted or added.

and to become the lifegivers
        of a past we come to celebrate
                and a future we dare to fashion!

WATERS OF THE EARTH[1]

In the beginning
    God's waters broke
        and a world was born
Then God laughed and the rains fell:
   the oceans filled and rivers ran home
      puddles pooled into lakes
         and brooks and streams veined their way across the earth.
The seasons danced in circles
    as people sang and children played
and men and women fell into each other's lives.
      Oh, it was paradise!

Then a tree was robbed,
    and the thirst began:

A stone crushed brother-life
a tower babbled at the sky
  and the thirst grew
    and the wilderness was born . . .
      The desert claimed the human soul
and would not let it go.

But God's Promise moved upon the waters:

        No more will your parched tongues seek water
        No more will the land cry for rain
        God's justice will rain on your daughters
        God's mercy will heal your sons' pain

---

1. The refrain can be set to a melody and sung by proclaimers and assembly together. Gestures can also be choreographed for the refrain, taught to the assembly prior to beginning of presentation and performed by all as refrain is spoken or sung.

Then came the longing
    and the journey . . .
        the seeking and the craving and the waiting:
The earth and her people united in pain
    they sighed out their prayers in dust-storms and darkness
        in deserts of exile, fatigue and in shame

Till a dove took the sky and ripped it in two
    and a cloud-voice thundered good news
        that the Promise was born, by a cousin baptized,
    and God's music was starting anew . . .

        No more will your parched tongues seek water
        No more will the land cry for rain
        God's justice will rain on your daughters
        God's mercy will heal your sons' pain

And the Promise went walking out into the desert
    and he tasted the thirst that was born there
        and the thirst wanted him to adore it
    but he stared in its eyes
        and the desert trembled and shook
            for its grip on the earth was about to be broken.

Then the fertile God's waters broke once again
    and they flowed from the side of the Promise
        on a table of pain where he lay to give birth

        he said,
        Come all you thirsty
        Come drink from a fountain of life-giving water
        God has birthed you an end to the thirst.

Then a wind was heard rushing
    tongues of fire were speaking
        bringing hope and announcing . . .

No more will your parched tongues seek water
No more will the land cry for rain
God's justice will rain on your daughters
God's mercy will heal your sons' pain

Before us this day God sets desert and fountain
and bids us to choose which one we will be:
God's life-giving water
or forever thirsty?

May our voices responding make a sound like the wind
like the rush and the flow of great waters:
Help us be water, make us part of the flow
make us fountains of thirst-quenching water.
Let us be rivers that irrigate deserts
that open the floodgates of peace;
Make us torrents that knock down walls that divide
that overwhelm hatred and grief.
Make us rivers of blessing, and rivers of life
make us springs of sweet tasting hope;
Make us oceans enormous, abundant and strong
and make the flow of our lives add new joy to the
song . . .

No more will your parched tongues seek water
No more will the land cry for rain
God's justice will rain on your daughters
God's mercy will heal your sons' pain

ON HOLY GROUND[1]

When it was time for her to be delivered
  God said,
"Let the earth bring forth!"
         And it happened.
The earth, bursting with God's seed,
      brought forth children in abundance.
She birthed every plant and every kind of tree;
        she crowded the oceans and the land
        with wild and creeping things—
    winged and monstrous creatures she brought forth.
And God's own image walked the earth.
Such wonders, wonders, wonders came to birth.

      Then a wind started blowing
        over, under, around.
      "Loose your shoes," it was saying,
        "let your feet be unbound,
      for the place where you stand is God's holy ground."

Then the earth closed her eyes to rest from her labors,
  and as sleep overcame her she started to dream.
She dreamed of a time when the earth was divided:
      her children were strangers
        to her and each other;
    they knew not their mother,
      nor their sisters and brothers,
    they knew not the love that was poured on the land.
They'd extinguished the light of the sky with their poisons,
      they'd clogged the earth's veins with all their debris.
They'd scraped, and they'd scoured, and raped their own mother,
    saying the measure of life is "What's best for me."

1. The refrain can be set to music and sung by proclaimers and assembly
together. Gestures can be choreographed for the refrain, taught to the assembly
prior to start of the presentation and performed by all as refrain is spoken or
sung.

How the earth wept
    and stirred as she slept
        she trembled and shook and awakened.
And she saw that the dream was not just a dream
    for her youth had indeed been forsaken.
        Her face now bore scars,
            her hair was supplanted,
        her bent back and hands bore sure signs of neglect.
With horror she learned not to take it for granted
    that children would show their own mother respect.

        Then a wind started blowing
            over, under, around.
        "Loose your shoes," it was saying,
            "let your feet be unbound,
        for the place where you stand is God's holy ground."

And the earth, like a mother too outraged to grieve,
called and spoke to the children of Adam and Eve.
    "The God who created entrusted to you
        a garden abundant and rich.
    But you've squandered your birthright,
        you've ravaged the land
        in the name of hungry ambition.
    You've built your dark towers that belch smoky darkness,
        washed your hands in the sweat of the poor and oppressed.
    Your eyes have turned green with greedy extortion;
        your knees will not bend to hallow the land.
    Your ears have grown deaf to lies and distortion
        and rampant injustice paralyzes your hands.
    Listen and hear the cry of the stranger.
        Right the wrongs done to your neighbor and land.
    Seek to reduce the imminent danger
        and restore to creation the order God planned."

Then a wind started blowing
over, under, around.
"Loose your shoes," it was saying,
"let your feet be unbound,
for the place where you stand is God's holy ground."

When the earth had chastised her much beloved children
she lay in exhaustion and fell off to sleep.

Then the merciful God gave her a dream
of a time when the world was united.
The dream of the earth was a dream of new birth
when injustice was dead and all wrongs had been righted.
Earth's children beat bombs into food for the poor
and the honor of all had, at last, been secured.

"Give your lives to the dream," the earth begged her children,
who rose up in joy-filled contrition.
"Yield to the call to be humble and small
and cherish God's wondrous creation."

"We will dream the dream," earth's children replied;
"we'll surrender to tender compassion.
We'll work on each problem till all answers we've tried
and see mercy's abundantly rationed.
We'll honor each other as sister and brother,
not forget that the earth is our mother.
And only in love will we try to compete
and not cease to outdo one another."

Then a wind started blowing
over, under, around.
"Loose your shoes," it was saying,
"let your feet be unbound,
for the place where you stand is God's holy ground."

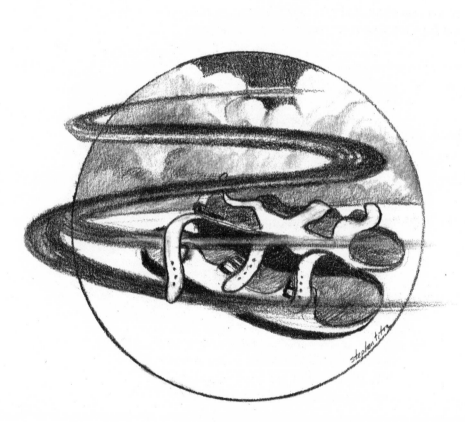

WOUNDED HEALERS[1]

We are catholics
    We are Americans
        We are wounded
            We are healers

We are
American Catholics
Wounded healers!

We are young and getting younger
Old and getting wiser

From the farm belt and the sun belt
The rust belt
And the tightened belt.
    From Florida to Kansas
    Albuquerque to Kalamazoo
    Wandering Indiana and shuffling off to Buffalo
        —With Georgia on our minds

Swimming the 10,000 lakes
    Catching cold in my kind of town
Battling indigestion in the big apple
    And depression in the lone star
Climbing the purple mountains and sailing the amber waves

1. This proclamation was commissioned by the Catholic Health Association of America for the celebration that included Pope John Paul II's address to the organization in Phoenix, Arizona during his 1987 pastoral visit to the United States. Special thanks to Sr. Juliana Casey, IHM and the drafters of the document, "We Are American Catholics" that resulted from the 1987 National Consultation with the Laity.

I am a nurse,
A radiologist
A dietician
And an orderly

I check pulses and temperatures, blood pressure
and bed pans
    I wrench my back and prick my finger
And dispense pills that cure anything except my tired feet
    I change sheets and mop floors
I suture wounds for crying babies, drunken teens and brave fathers
    I go off-duty praying she'll still be here when I come back on
I put bones back in their places
and make plaster prisons to hold them till they're whole
    I call families to inform them that one member won't be coming
    home
I sit in an office and operate
    on budgets
I worry
        I laugh
                I complain
I pray . . . I sleep
      and pray again
I sing in the hallways and slip down the stairs

I am a wounded healer
An American
A Catholic
A Protestant
A Jew
A Hindu
A Buddhist
An atheist
And a masochist

In every shade and color
     from coffee
     to cream
     and every blending in between
          Yellow as the sun
          and red as a sun-burn
Speaking Hindi, Tagalog, Korean, Arabic, French, and Chinese
     and English . . . with an accent

Building clinics and hospitals
Medical centers and empires
     And communities

Powerful, yes
     but not invincible
Arrogant, yes
     but humbled by hard work
Jaded, sometimes
     but awed by each new life

Hearing the names some call us:
     "Cynical!"
          "Callous!"
               "Insensitive!"
                    "Profiteering!"
But still secure when looking in the mirror

We make mistakes
But we're still learning
And still smiling back

High tech,
     State-of-the-art,
          And as up-to-date as tomorrow's news
But mindful of our roots
And thankful, too

We are wounded healers
        and we have a story to tell.
My story—
     Our story—
         God's story!

A story about remembering
     God's story
     Our story
And as we remember
       we are blessed again
         and are committed again
       And we hear again the echoes
         and touch again the miracles
       and know
               again
                     the glory of God's love

WE ARE GOD'S GLORY![1]

We are the new Jerusalem
We are the bride
We are God's dwelling on earth
    beautiful as a runaway in the arms of her mother
We are the glory of God
    proclaimed in many colors
We are the glory of God
    spoken in many languages

We are the boldness . . .
    the courage of God
We are God's power erupting in joy
We are God's springtime
    greening the carpet that covers the earth;
    recalling the robins,
        inviting them home,
        with promise of warmth in the land of their birth

We are the song God sings in the morning
    when she first awakens and stretches her arms
We are the lullaby God sings in the darkness
    when he senses that fear has gone on the prowl

We are God's song,
    God's favorite song
We are lyrics and melody
    blended in harmonies new;
singing laughter and pain, sunshine and rain,
    and dancing them, too!

Stephen Fitts

---

1. This proclamation lends itself to being danced by a solo dancer. Instrumental music can play in the background as the reader speaks and the dancer's movement interprets the lines.

We are the good news proclaimed to all nations
    We are the nations who long for God's reign

We are the rain that flows from God's eyes
    when love is not free, when free people don't love
We are God's rain baptizing the earth;
    washing its face and watering its dreams
We are God's mercy healing the wounded,
    dressing the naked, and burying the dead

We are God's knowledge shared with the unlearned
And we are God's body
    feeding the hungers of the living and dead
We are the proof that God is a surgeon
    working on hearts and making them new

We are God's joy
    and God's celebration
We are God's pulse proving God is alive

We are God's lunatic notion,
      tenaciously claiming,
    that hope with its feathers has not taken wing
We are God's madness, seriously saying,
    that while there is life
      our hearts still can sing!

We are God's passion proving, insanely,
    even death does not end the good we can do

We are God's glory, proclaimed and proclaiming:
in God we are glorified; in us, God is too!